CLARINET

101 HIT SONGS

T0066466

Available for
FLUTE, CLARINET, ALTO SAX, TENOR SAX, TRUMPET,
HORN, TROMBONE, VIOLIN, VIOLA, CELLO

ISBN 978-1-4950-7529-2

HAL•LEONARD®

7777 W. BLUEMOUND RD. P.O. BOX 13819 MILWAUKEE, WI 53213

For all works contained herein:
Unauthorized copying, arranging, adapting, recording, Internet posting, public performance,
or other distribution of the printed music in this publication is an infringement of copyright.
Infringers are liable under the law.

Visit Hal Leonard Online at
www.halleonard.com

CONTENTS

4 All About That Bass

6 All of Me

5 Amazed

8 Apologize

10 Bad Day

12 Bad Romance

9 Beautiful

14 Beautiful Day

16 Beautiful in My Eyes

17 Because I Love You (The Postman Song)

18 Believe

20 Brave

22 Breakaway

24 Breathe

19 Butterfly Kisses

26 Call Me Maybe

28 Candle in the Wind 1997

29 Change the World

30 Chasing Cars

31 The Climb

32 Clocks

34 Countdown

36 Cruise

38 Cryin'

40 Die a Happy Man

42 Dilemma

33 Don't Know Why

44 Drift Away

46 Drops of Jupiter (Tell Me)

48 Fallin'

45 Fields of Gold

50 Firework

52 Foolish Games

54 Forever and for Always

56 Friends in Low Places

57 From a Distance

58 Genie in a Bottle

60 Get Lucky

62 Hello

64 Here and Now

66 Hero

68 Hey, Soul Sister

70 Ho Hey

72 Hold On, We're Going Home

74 Home

76 The House That Built Me

78 How Am I Supposed to Live Without You

61 How to Save a Life

80 I Finally Found Someone

82 I Gotta Feeling

84 I Kissed a Girl

86 I Swear

87 I Will Remember You

88 Jar of Hearts

90 Just the Way You Are

96 Let It Go

92 Lips of an Angel

94 Little Talks

98 Losing My Religion

100 Love Song

102 Love Story

104 More Than Words

97 Need You Now

106 No One

108 100 Years

110 The Power of Love

109 Rehab

112 Roar

113 Rolling in the Deep

114 Royals

115 Save the Best for Last

116 Say Something

118 Secrets

117 Shake It Off

120 She Will Be Loved

121 Smells Like Teen Spirit

122 Something to Talk About
(Let's Give Them Something to Talk About)

124 Stacy's Mom

126 Stay

123 Stay with Me

128 Stronger (What Doesn't Kill You)

130 Tears in Heaven

131 Teenage Dream

132 Thinking Out Loud

134 This Love

135 A Thousand Years

136 Till the World Ends

138 Uptown Funk

140 Viva La Vida

142 Waiting on the World to Change

144 We Belong Together

143 We Can't Stop

146 We Found Love

147 What Makes You Beautiful

148 When You Say Nothing at All

150 Yeah!

149 You Raise Me Up

152 You Were Meant for Me

154 You're Beautiful

155 You're Still the One

156 You've Got a Friend in Me

ALL ABOUT THAT BASS

Clarinet

Words and Music by KEVIN KADISH
and MEGHAN TRAINOR

Copyright © 2014 Sony/ATV Music Publishing LLC, Over-Thought Under-Appreciated Songs, Year Of The Dog Music,
a division of Big Yellow Dog, LLC and MTrain Music
All Rights on behalf of Sony/ATV Music Publishing LLC and Over-Thought Under-Appreciated Songs Administered by
Sony/ATV Music Publishing LLC, 424 Church Street, Suite 1200, Nashville, TN 37219
All Rights on behalf of Year Of The Dog Music, a division of Big Yellow Dog, LLC and MTrain Music Administered by Words & Music
International Coyright Secured   All Rights Reserved

AMAZED

Clarinet

Words and Music by MARV GREEN,
CHRIS LINDSEY and AIMEE MAYO

Copyright © 1998, 1999 by Universal Music - Careers, Silverkiss Music Publishing, Reservoir Media Management, Inc. and Golden Wheat Music
All Rights for Silverkiss Music Publishing Administered by Universal Music - Careers
All Rights for Reservoir Media Music Administered by Reservoir Media Management, Inc.
Reservoir Media Music Administered by Alfred Music
All Rights for Golden Wheat Music Administered by Round Hill Music LP/Big Loud Songs
International Copyright Secured All Rights Reserved

ALL OF ME

CLARINET

Words and Music by JOHN STEPHENS
and TOBY GAD

Copyright © 2013 John Legend Publishing, EMI April Music Inc. and Gad Songs, LLC
All Rights for John Legend Publishing Administered by BMG Rights Management (US) LLC
All Rights for EMI April Music Inc. and Gad Songs, LLC Administered by
Sony/ATV Music Publishing LLC, 424 Church Street, Suite 1200, Nashville, TN 37219
All Rights Reserved   Used by Permission

APOLOGIZE

CLARINET

Words and Music by
RYAN TEDDER

Copyright © 2007 Sony/ATV Music Publishing LLC, Midnite Miracle Music and Velvet Hammer Music
All Rights Administered by Sony/ATV Music Publishing LLC, 424 Church Street, Suite 1200, Nashville, TN 37219
International Copyright Secured   All Rights Reserved

BEAUTIFUL

Clarinet

Words and Music by
LINDA PERRY

Moderately slow

Copyright © 2002 Sony/ATV Music Publishing LLC and Stuck In The Throat Music
All Rights Administered by Sony/ATV Music Publishing LLC, 424 Church Street, Suite 1200, Nashville, TN 37219
International Copyright Secured   All Rights Reserved

BAD DAY

CLARINET

Words and Music by
DANIEL POWTER

Copyright © 2005 Song 6 Music
All Rights Administered by BMG Rights Management (US) LLC
All Rights Reserved   Used by Permission

D.S. al Coda

CODA

BAD ROMANCE

CLARINET

Words and Music by STEFANI GERMANOTTA
and NADIR KHAYAT

Copyright © 2009 Sony/ATV Music Publishing LLC and House Of Gaga Publishing Inc.
All Rights Administered by Sony/ATV Music Publishing LLC, 424 Church Street, Suite 1200, Nashville, TN 37219
International Copyright Secured   All Rights Reserved

BEAUTIFUL DAY

CLARINET

Words by BONO
Music by U2

Copyright © 2000 UNIVERSAL - POLYGRAM INTERNATIONAL MUSIC PUBLISHING B.V.
All Rights in the United States and Canada Controlled and Administered by UNIVERSAL - POLYGRAM INTERNATIONAL PUBLISHING, INC.
All Rights Reserved   Used by Permission

BEAUTIFUL IN MY EYES

CLARINET

Words and Music by
JOSHUA KADISON

Moderately slow

Copyright © 1992 EMI Blackwood Music Inc., Joshuasongs and Seymour Glass Music
All Rights Administered by Sony/ATV Music Publishing LLC, 424 Church Street, Suite 1200, Nashville, TN 37219
International Copyright Secured   All Rights Reserved

BECAUSE I LOVE YOU
(The Postman Song)

CLARINET

Words and Music by
WARREN BROOKS

Slowly

Copyright © 1989 R2M Music and Songs Of Lastrada
All Rights Administered by BMG Rights Management (US) LLC
All Rights Reserved   Used by Permission

BELIEVE

CLARINET

Words and Music by BRIAN HIGGINS,
STUART McLENNEN, PAUL BARRY,
STEPHEN TORCH, MATT GRAY
and TIM POWELL

Copyright © 1998 PB SONGS LTD., XENOMANIA MUSIC and BMG RIGHTS MANAGEMENT (UK) LTD.
All Rights for PB SONGS LTD. Controlled and Administered by UNIVERSAL - POLYGRAM INTERNATIONAL PUBLISHING, INC.
All Rights for XENOMANIA MUSIC Administered by WB MUSIC CORP.
All Rights Reserved   Used by Permission

BUTTERFLY KISSES

CLARINET

Words and Music by BOB CARLISLE
and RANDY THOMAS

Copyright © 1996 UNIVERSAL - POLYGRAM INTERNATIONAL PUBLISHING, INC. and DESIGNER MUSIC (SESAC)
All Rights for DESIGNER MUSIC Admin. at CAPITOLCMGPUBLISHING.COM
All Rights Reserved   Used by Permission

BRAVE

CLARINET

Words and Music by SARA BAREILLES
and JACK ANTONOFF

Moderately

Copyright © 2013 Sony/ATV Music Publishing LLC, Tiny Bear Music and Ducky Donath Music
All Rights Administered by Sony/ATV Music Publishing LLC, 424 Church Street, Suite 1200, Nashville, TN 37219
International Copyright Secured   All Rights Reserved

To Coda ⊕

D.S. al Coda

CODA ⊕

BREAKAWAY

from THE PRINCESS DIARIES 2: ROYAL ENGAGEMENT

Clarinet

Words and Music by BRIDGET BENENATE,
AVRIL LAVIGNE and MATTHEW GERRARD

Copyright © 2004 Music Of Windswept, Friends Of Seagulls Music Publishing, Almo Music Corp.,
Avril Lavigne Publishing Ltd., WB Music Corp. and G Matt Music
All Rights for Music Of Windswept and Friends Of Seagulls Music Publishing Administered by BMG Rights Management (US) LLC
All Rights for Avril Lavigne Publishing Ltd. Controlled and Administered by Almo Music Corp.
All Rights for G Matt Music Administered by WB Music Corp.
All Rights Reserved   Used by Permission

BREATHE

CLARINET

Words and Music by HOLLY LAMAR
and STEPHANIE BENTLEY

Copyright © 1999 Spirit Catalog Holdings, S.á.r.l., Universal - Songs Of PolyGram International, Inc. and Hopechest Music
All Rights on for Spirit Catalog Holdings, S.á.r.l. Controlled and Administered by Spirit Two Nashville
All Rights for Hopechest Music Controlled and Administered by Universal - Songs Of PolyGram International, Inc.
All Rights Reserved   Used by Permission

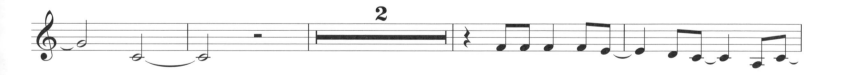

CALL ME MAYBE

CLARINET

Words and Music by CARLY RAE JEPSEN,
JOSHUA RAMSAY and TAVISH CROWE

Copyright © 2011 UNIVERSAL MUSIC CORP., JEPSEN MUSIC PUBLISHING, BMG GOLD SONGS, CROWE MUSIC INC.,
BMG PLATINUM SONGS and REGULAR MONKEY PRODUCTIONS
All Rights for JEPSEN MUSIC PUBLISHING Controlled and Administered by UNIVERSAL MUSIC CORP.
All Rights for BMG GOLD SONGS, CROWE MUSIC INC., BMG PLATINUM SONGS and REGULAR MONKEY PRODUCTIONS
Administered by BMG RIGHTS MANAGEMENT (US) LLC
All Rights Reserved   Used by Permission

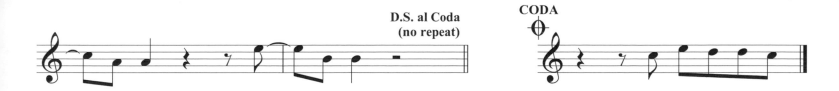

CANDLE IN THE WIND 1997

Clarinet

Words and Music by ELTON JOHN
and BERNIE TAUPIN

Slowly, in 2

Copyright © 1973, 1997 UNIVERSAL/DICK JAMES MUSIC LTD.
Copyright Renewed
All Rights in the United States and Canada Controlled and Administered by UNIVERSAL - SONGS OF POLYGRAM INTERNATIONAL, INC.
All Rights Reserved   Used by Permission

CHANGE THE WORLD

featured on the Motion Picture Soundtrack PHENOMENON

Clarinet

Words and Music by WAYNE KIRKPATRICK,
GORDON KENNEDY and TOMMY SIMS

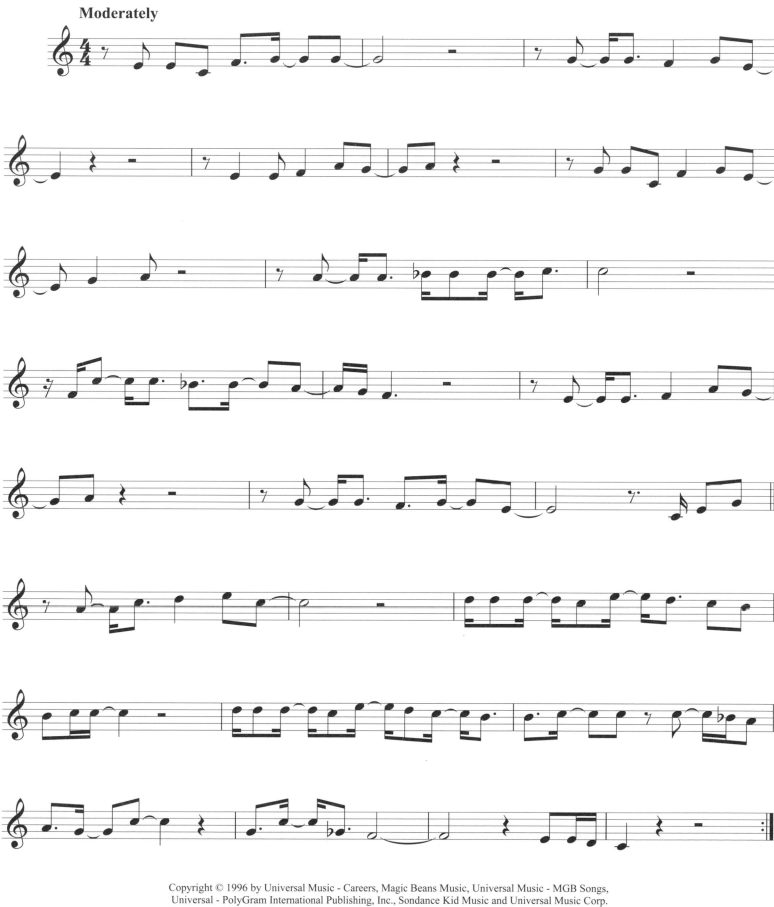

Copyright © 1996 by Universal Music - Careers, Magic Beans Music, Universal Music - MGB Songs,
Universal - PolyGram International Publishing, Inc., Sondance Kid Music and Universal Music Corp.
All Rights for Magic Beans Music Administered by Universal Music - Careers
All Rights for Sondance Kid Music Controlled and Administered by Universal - PolyGram International Publishing, Inc.
International Copyright Secured   All Rights Reserved

CHASING CARS

Clarinet

Words and Music by GARY LIGHTBODY,
TOM SIMPSON, PAUL WILSON,
JONATHAN QUINN and NATHAN CONNOLLY

Copyright © 2006 UNIVERSAL MUSIC PUBLISHING BL LTD.
All Rights in the U.S. and Canada Controlled and Administered by UNIVERSAL - SONGS OF POLYGRAM INTERNATIONAL, INC.
All Rights Reserved   Used by Permission

THE CLIMB

from HANNAH MONTANA: THE MOVIE

Clarinet

Words and Music by JESSI ALEXANDER
and JON MABE

© 2007, 2009 Vistaville Music, Hopeless Rose Music, Music Of Stage Three and Mabe It Big
All Rights for Hopeless Rose Music Administered by Vistaville Music
All Rights for Music Of Stage Three and Mabe it Big Administered by BMG Rights Management (US) LLC
All Rights Reserved.   Used by Permission.

CLOCKS

CLARINET

Words and Music by GUY BERRYMAN,
JON BUCKLAND, WILL CHAMPION
and CHRIS MARTIN

Copyright © 2002 by Universal Music Publishing MGB Ltd.
All Rights in the United States Administered by Universal Music - MGB Songs
International Copyright Secured   All Rights Reserved

DON'T KNOW WHY

CLARINET

Words and Music by
JESSE HARRIS

Copyright © 2002 Sony/ATV Music Publishing LLC and Beanly Songs
All Rights Administered by Sony/ATV Music Publishing LLC, 424 Church Street, Suite 1200, Nashville, TN 37219
International Copyright Secured   All Rights Reserved

COUNTDOWN

Clarinet

Words and Music by BEYONCÉ KNOWLES,
CAINON LAMB, JULIE FROST, MICHAEL BIVINS,
ESTHER DEAN, TERIUS NASH, SHEA TAYLOR,
NATHAN MORRIS and WANYA MORRIS

© 2011 EMI APRIL MUSIC INC., B-DAY PUBLISHING, CAINON'S LAND MUSIC PUBLISHING, TOTALLY FAMOUS MUSIC,
UNIVERSAL MUSIC CORP., BIV TEN PUBLISHING, PEERMUSIC III, LTD., DAT DAMN DEAN MUSIC, 2412 LLC,
2082 MUSIC PUBLISHING, DLJ SONGS and MIKE TEN PUBLISHING, INC.
All Rights for B-DAY PUBLISHING, CAINON'S LAND MUSIC PUBLISHING and TOTALLY FAMOUS MUSIC
Controlled and Administered by EMI APRIL MUSIC INC.
All Rights for BIV TEN PUBLISHING Controlled and Administered by UNIVERSAL MUSIC CORP.
All Rights for DAT DAMN DEAN MUSIC and 2412 LLC Administered by PEERMUSIC III,, LTD.
All Rights for 2082 MUSIC PUBLISHING Administered by WB MUSIC CORP.
All Rights Reserved   International Copyright Secured   Used by Permission
- contains sample of "Uhh Ahh"

2nd time, D.C. al Coda

CODA

CRUISE

Clarinet

Words and Music by CHASE RICE,
TYLER HUBBARD, BRIAN KELLEY,
JOEY MOI and JESSE RICE

Moderately, in 2

Copyright © 2012 Sony/ATV Music Publishing LLC, Dack Janiels Publishing, Big Loud Mountain, Big Red Toe,
Deep Fried Dreams and Artist Revolution Publishing
All Rights on behalf of Sony/ATV Music Publishing LLC and Dack Janiels Publishing Administered by
Sony/ATV Music Publishing LLC, 424 Church Street, Suite 1200, Nashville, TN 37219
All Rights on behalf of Big Loud Mountain, Big Red Toe and Deep Fried Dreams Administered by Big Loud Bucks
All Rights on behalf of Artist Revolution Publishing Administered by ole
International Copyright Secured   All Rights Reserved

CRYIN'

CLARINET

Words and Music by STEVEN TYLER,
JOE PERRY and TAYLOR RHODES

Moderately slow, in 2

Copyright © 1993 Juju Rhythms, Universal Music Corp., T. Rhodes Songs and Primary Wave Steven Tyler
All Rights on behalf of Juju Rhythms Administered by Sony/ATV Music Publishing LLC, 424 Church Street, Suite 1200, Nashville, TN 37219
All Rights on behalf of T. Rhodes Songs Administered by Universal Music Corp.
All Rights on behalf of Primary Wave Steven Tyler Administered by BMG Rights Management (US) LLC
International Copyright Secured   All Rights Reserved

DIE A HAPPY MAN

Clarinet

Words and Music by THOMAS RHETT,
JOE SPARGUR and SEAN DOUGLAS

Copyright © 2015 EMI Blackwood Music Inc., Cricket On The Line, Music Of Big Deal, Brodsky Spensive Publishing,
Nice Life, Warner-Tamerlane Publishing Corp. and Eastman Pond Publishing
All Rights on behalf of EMI Blackwood Music Inc. and Cricket On The Line Administered by
Sony/ATV Music Publishing LLC, 424 Church Street, Suite 1200, Nashville, TN 37219
All Rights on behalf of Music Of Big Deal, Brodsky Spensive Publishing and Nice Life Administered by BMG Rights Management (US) LLC
All Rights on behalf of Eastman Pond Publishing Administered by Warner-Tamerlane Publishing Corp.
International Copyright Secured   All Rights Reserved

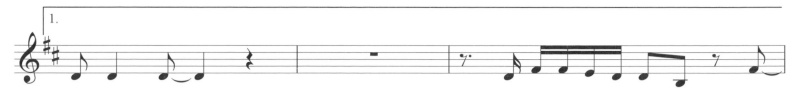

DILEMMA

CLARINET

Words and Music by CORNELL HAYNES,
ANTWON MAKER, KENNETH GAMBLE
and BUNNY SIGLER

Copyright © 2002 UNIVERSAL MUSIC - MGB SONGS, JACKIE FROST MUSIC, INC., WARNER-TAMERLANE PUBLISHING CORP. and SUGA SHACK MUSIC
All Rights for JACKIE FROST MUSIC, INC. Administered by UNIVERSAL MUSIC - MGB SONGS
All Rights Reserved   Used by Permission

Fine

2nd time, D.S. al Fine

DRIFT AWAY

CLARINET

Words and Music by
MENTOR WILLIAMS

Copyright © 1972 ALMO MUSIC CORP.
Copyright Renewed
All Rights Reserved   Used by Permission

FIELDS OF GOLD

CLARINET

Music and Lyrics by
STING

Copyright © 1993 Steerpike Ltd.
All Rights Administered by Sony/ATV Music Publishing LLC, 424 Church Street, Suite 1200, Nashville, TN 37219
International Copyright Secured   All Rights Reserved

DROPS OF JUPITER
(Tell Me)

CLARINET

Words and Music by PAT MONAHAN,
JAMES STAFFORD, ROBERT HOTCHKISS,
CHARLES COLIN and SCOTT UNDERWOOD

Copyright © 2000 EMI April Music Inc. and Blue Lamp Music
All Rights Administered by Sony/ATV Music Publishing LLC, 424 Church Street, Suite 1200, Nashville, TN 37219
International Copyright Secured   All Rights Reserved

D.S. al Coda

CODA

FALLIN'

CLARINET

Words and Music by
ALICIA KEYS

© 2001 EMI APRIL MUSIC INC. and LELLOW PRODUCTIONS
All Rights Controlled and Administered by EMI APRIL MUSIC INC.
All Rights Reserved   International Copyright Secured   Used by Permission

FIREWORK

Clarinet

Words and Music by KATY PERRY,
MIKKEL ERIKSEN, TOR ERIK HERMANSEN,
ESTHER DEAN and SANDY WILHELM

Moderately

© 2010 WHEN I'M RICH YOU'LL BE MY BITCH, EMI MUSIC PUBLISHING LTD., PEERMUSIC III, LTD.,
DAT DAMN DEAN MUSIC, 2412 LLC and DIPIU SRL
All Rights for WHEN I'M RICH YOU'LL BE MY BITCH Administered by WB MUSIC CORP.
All Rights for EMI MUSIC PUBLISHING LTD. in the U. S. and Canada Controlled and Administered by EMI APRIL MUSIC INC.
All Rights for DAT DAMN DEAN MUSIC and 2412 LLC Controlled and Administered by PEERMUSIC III, LTD.
All Rights for DIPIU SRL Administered by DOWNTOWN DMP SONGS
All Rights Reserved   Used by Permission

FOOLISH GAMES

CLARINET

Words and Music by
JEWEL KILCHER

Copyright © 1995 Wiggly Tooth Music
All Rights Administered by Downtown DLJ Songs
All Rights Reserved   Used by Permission

FOREVER AND FOR ALWAYS

CLARINET

Words and Music by SHANIA TWAIN
and R.J. LANGE

Moderately, in 2

Copyright © 2002 LOON ECHO, INC. and OUT OF POCKET PRODUCTIONS LTD.
All Rights for LOON ECHO, INC. Controlled and Administered by SONGS OF UNIVERSAL, INC.
All Rights for OUT OF POCKET PRODUCTIONS LTD. in the U.S. and Canada Controlled and Administered by
UNIVERSAL - POLYGRAM INTERNATIONAL PUBLISHING, INC.
All Rights Reserved   Used by Permission

FRIENDS IN LOW PLACES

Clarinet

Words and Music by DeWAYNE BLACKWELL
and EARL BUD LEE

Copyright © 1990 by Universal Music - Careers and Sony/ATV Music Publishing LLC
All Rights on behalf of Sony/ATV Music Publishing LLC Administered by
Sony/ATV Music Publishing LLC, 424 Church Street, Suite 1200, Nashville, TN 37219
International Copyright Secured   All Rights Reserved

FROM A DISTANCE

Clarinet

Words and Music by
JULIE GOLD

Copyright © 1986, 1987 Julie Gold Music (BMI) and Wing & Wheel Music (BMI)
Wing & Wheel Music Administered Worldwide by Irving Music, Inc.
International Copyright Secured   All Rights Reserved

GENIE IN A BOTTLE

Clarinet

Words and Music by STEVE KIPNER,
DAVID FRANK and PAMELA SHEYNE

Copyright © 1997 EMI April Music Inc., Griff Griff Music - EMI Catalog and Appletreesongs Ltd.
All Rights for EMI April Music Inc. and Griff Griff Music - EMI Catalog Administered by
Sony/ATV Music Publishing LLC, 424 Church Street, Suite 1200, Nashville, TN 37219
International Copyright Secured   All Rights Reserved

GET LUCKY

Clarinet

Words and Music by THOMAS BANGALTER,
GUY MANUEL HOMEM CHRISTO, NILE RODGERS
and PHARRELL WILLIAMS

Copyright © 2013 Imagem CV, XLC Music, EMI April Music Inc. and More Water From Nazareth
All Rights on behalf of XLC Music, EMI April Music Inc. and More Water From Nazareth Administered by
Sony/ATV Music Publishing LLC, 424 Church Street, Suite 1200, Nashville, TN 37219
All Rights Reserved   Used by Permission

HOW TO SAVE A LIFE

Clarinet

Words and Music by JOSEPH KING
and ISAAC SLADE

© 2005 EMI APRIL MUSIC INC. and AARON EDWARDS PUBLISHING
All Rights Controlled and Administered by EMI APRIL MUSIC INC.
All Rights Reserved   International Copyright Secured   Used by Permission

HELLO

CLARINET

Words and Music by ADELE ADKINS
and GREG KURSTIN

Copyright © 2015 MELTED STONE PUBLISHING LTD., EMI APRIL MUSIC INC. and KURSTIN MUSIC
All Rights for MELTED STONE PUBLISHING LTD. in the U.S. and Canada Administered by
UNIVERSAL - SONGS OF POLYGRAM INTERNATIONAL, INC.
All Rights for EMI APRIL MUSIC INC. and KURSTIN MUSIC Administered by
SONY/ATV MUSIC PUBLISHING LLC, 424 Church Street, Suite 1200, Nashville, TN 37219
All Rights Reserved   Used by Permission

HERE AND NOW

Clarinet

Words and Music by TERRY STEELE
and DAVID ELLIOT

© 1989 EMI APRIL MUSIC INC., OLLIE BROWN SUGAR MUSIC, UNIVERSAL MUSIC CORP. and D.L.E. MUSIC
All Rights for OLLIE BROWN SUGAR MUSIC throughout the World Controlled and Administered by EMI APRIL MUSIC INC.
All Rights for D.L.E. MUSIC in the U.S. and Canada Controlled and Administered by UNIVERSAL MUSIC CORP.
All Rights for D.L.E. MUSIC in the World excluding the U.S. and Canada Controlled and Administered by EMI APRIL MUSIC INC.
All Rights Reserved   International Copyright Secured   Used by Permission

HERO

CLARINET

Words and Music by ENRIQUE IGLESIAS,
PAUL BARRY and MARK TAYLOR

Copyright © 2001 EMI April Music Inc., Enrique Iglesias Music, Rive Droite and Metrophonic Music
All Rights on behalf of EMI April Music Inc. and Enrique Iglesias Music Administered by
Sony/ATV Music Publishing LLC, 424 Church Street, Suite 1200, Nashville, TN 37219
All Rights on behalf of Metrophonic Music in the U.S. and Canada Controlled and Administered by
Universal - PolyGram International Publishing, Inc.
International Copyright Secured   All Rights Reserved

HEY, SOUL SISTER

CLARINET

Words and Music by PAT MONAHAN,
ESPEN LIND and AMUND BJORKLUND

Copyright © 2009 EMI April Music Inc., Blue Lamp Music and Stellar Songs Ltd.
All Rights Administered by Sony/ATV Music Publishing LLC, 424 Church Street, Suite 1200, Nashville, TN 37219
International Copyright Secured   All Rights Reserved

HO HEY

CLARINET

Words and Music by JEREMY FRAITES
and WESLEY SCHULTZ

Copyright © 2011 The Lumineers
All Rights Exclusively Administered by Songs Of Kobalt Music Publishing
All Rights Reserved   Used by Permission

HOLD ON, WE'RE GOING HOME

CLARINET

Words and Music by AUBREY GRAHAM,
PAUL JEFFERIES, NOAH SHEBIB,
JORDAN ULLMAN and MAJID AL-MASKATI

© 2013 EMI APRIL MUSIC INC., IS LOVE AND ABOVE, EMI MUSIC PUBLISHING LTD., NYAN KING MUSIC INC.,
MAVOR AND MOSES PUBLISHING LLC d/b/a RONCESVALLES MUSIC PUBLISHING, WB MUSIC CORP.,
OTEK PUBLISHING ASCAP PUB DESIGNEE, JORDAN ULLMAN ASCAP PUB DESIGNEE and MAJID AL-MASKATI ASCAP PUB DESIGNEE
All Rights for IS LOVE AND ABOVE Controlled and Administered by EMI APRIL MUSIC INC.
All Rights for EMI MUSIC PUBLISHING LTD. and NYAN KING MUSIC INC. in the U.S. and Canada
Controlled and Administered by EMI APRIL MUSIC INC.
All Rights for MAVOR AND MOSES PUBLISHING, LLC d/b/a RONCEVALLES MUSIC PUBLISHING Administered by
KOBALT SONGS MUSIC PUBLISHING
All Rights for OTEK PUBLISHING ASCAP PUB DESIGNEE, JORDAN ULLMAN ASCAP PUB DESIGNEE and
MAJID AL-MASKATI ASCAP PUB DESIGNEE Administered by WB MUSIC CORP.
All Rights Reserved   International Copyright Secured   Used by Permission

HOME

CLARINET

Words and Music by GREG HOLDEN
and DREW PEARSON

Moderately, in 2

© 2012 FALLEN ART MUSIC, DREWYEAH MUSIC and SONGS OF PULSE RECORDING
All Rights for FALLEN ART MUSIC Administered by WB MUSIC CORP.
All Rights for DREWYEAH MUSIC Administered by SONGS OF PULSE RECORDING
All Rights Reserved   Used by Permission

THE HOUSE THAT BUILT ME

Clarinet

Words and Music by TOM DOUGLAS
and ALLEN SHAMBLIN

Moderately, in 2

Copyright © 2009 Sony/ATV Music Publishing LLC, Tomdouglasmusic and Built On Rock Music
All Rights on behalf of Sony/ATV Music Publishing LLC and Tomdouglasmusic Administered by
Sony/ATV Music Publishing LLC, 424 Church Street, Suite 1200, Nashville, TN 37219
All Rights on behalf of Built On Rock Music Administered by ClearBox Rights
International Copyright Secured   All Rights Reserved

HOW AM I SUPPOSED TO LIVE WITHOUT YOU

CLARINET

Words and Music by MICHAEL BOLTON
and DOUG JAMES

© 1983 EMI APRIL MUSIC INC., IS HOT MUSIC and EMI BLACKWOOD MUSIC INC.
All Rights for IS HOT MUSIC Controlled and Administered by EMI APRIL MUSIC INC.
All Rights Reserved   International Copyright Secured   Used by Permission

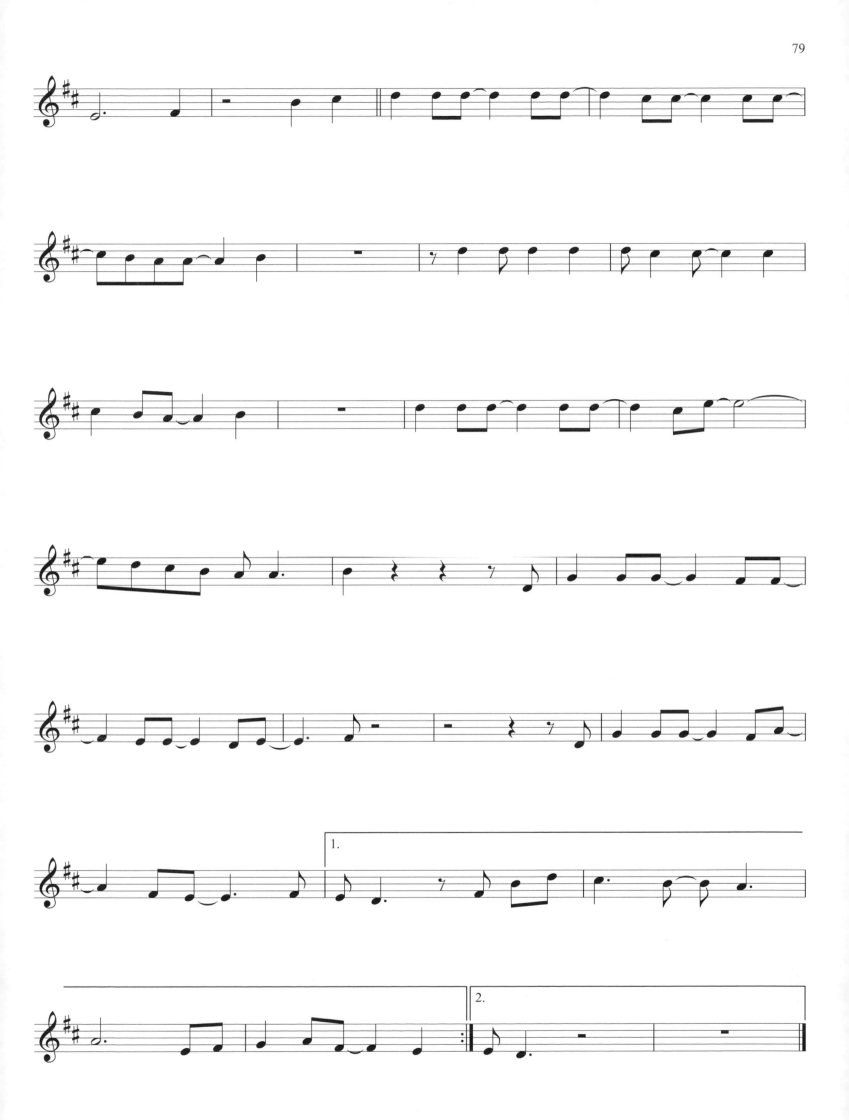

I FINALLY FOUND SOMEONE

from THE MIRROR HAS TWO FACES

Clarinet

Words and Music by BARBRA STREISAND,
MARVIN HAMLISCH, R.J. LANGE
and BRYAN ADAMS

Copyright © 1996 Emanuel Music, ole Team Sports Music, Out Of Pocket Productions Ltd. and Badmas Music Ltd.
All Rights on behalf of ole Team Sports Music Administered by Sony/ATV Music Publishing LLC, 424 Church Street, Suite 1200, Nashville, TN 37219
All Rights on behalf of Out Of Pocket Productions Ltd. in the United States and Canada Administered by
Universal - PolyGram International Publishing, Inc.
International Copyright Secured   All Rights Reserved

I GOTTA FEELING

CLARINET

Words and Music by WILL ADAMS,
ALLAN PINEDA, JAIME GOMEZ, STACY FERGUSON,
DAVID GUETTA and FREDERIC RIESTERER

Moderately fast

Copyright © 2009 BMG Sapphire Songs (BMI), Will.I.Am Music Inc. (BMI), Jeepney Music Publishing (BMI), Tab Magnetic Publishing (BMI),
EMI April Music Inc. (ASCAP), Headphone Junkie Publishing (ASCAP), Square Rivoli Publishing (SACEM) and Rister Editions (SACEM)
Worldwide Rights for BMG Sapphire Songs, Will.I.Am Music Inc., Jeepney Music Publishing and Tab Magnetic Publishing
Administered by BMG Rights Management (US) LLC
All Rights for Headphone Junkie Publishing Controlled and Administered by EMI April Music Inc.
All Rights for Square Rivoli Publishing and Rister Editions in the U.S. Administered by Shapiro, Bernstein & Co. Inc.
International Copyright Secured   All Rights Reserved

I KISSED A GIRL

CLARINET

Words and Music by KATY PERRY,
CATHY DENNIS, MAX MARTIN
and LUKASZ GOTTWALD

© 2008 WHEN I'M RICH YOU'LL BE MY BITCH, EMI MUSIC PUBLISHING LTD., PRESCRIPTION SONGS and KASZ MONEY PUBLISHING
All Rights for WHEN I'M RICH YOU'LL BE MY BITCH Administered by WB MUSIC CORP.
All Rights for EMI MUSIC PUBLISHING LTD. in the United States and Canada Controlled and Administered by EMI APRIL MUSIC INC.
All Rights for PRESCRIPTION SONGS and KASZ MONEY PUBLISHING Administered by KOBALT MUSIC PUBLISHING AMERICA, INC.
All Rights Reserved   Used by Permission

D.S. al Fine
(take 1st ending)

I SWEAR

CLARINET

Words and Music by FRANK MYERS
and GARY BAKER

Copyright © 1993 MPCA Lehsem Music, Publishing Two's Music and Morganactive Songs, Inc.
All Rights for MPCA Lehsem Music Administered by The Bicycle Music Company
International Copyright Secured   All Rights Reserved

I WILL REMEMBER YOU

Theme from THE BROTHERS McMULLEN

Clarinet

Words and Music by SARAH McLACHLAN,
SEAMUS EGAN and DAVE MERENDA

Copyright © 1995 Sony/ATV Music Publishing LLC, Tyde Music, Seamus Egan Music and T C F Music Publishing, Inc.
All Rights on behalf of Sony/ATV Music Publishing LLC and Tyde Music Administered by
Sony/ATV Music Publishing LLC, 424 Church Street, Suite 1200, Nashville, TN 37219
All Rights on behalf of Seamus Egan Music Administered by Fox Film Music Corp.
International Copyright Secured   All Rights Reserved

JAR OF HEARTS

Clarinet

Words and Music by BARRETT YERETSIAN,
CHRISTINA PERRI and DREW LAWRENCE

Copyright © 2010, 2011 BMG Rights Management (UK) Ltd., Philosophy Of Sound Publishing,
Miss Perri Lane Publishing, WB Music Corp. and Piggy Dog Music
All Rights for BMG Rights Management (UK) Ltd. and Philosophy Of Sound Publishing Administered by BMG Rights Management (US) LLC
All Rights for Miss Perri Lane Publishing Administered by Songs Of Kobalt Music Publishing
All Rights for Piggy Dog Music Administered by WB Music Corp.
All Rights Reserved   Used by Permission

JUST THE WAY YOU ARE

CLARINET

Words and Music by BRUNO MARS,
ARI LEVINE, PHILIP LAWRENCE,
KHARI CAIN and KHALIL WALTON

Moderately

© 2009, 2010 BMG FIREFLY, MARSFORCE MUSIC, BMG GOLD SONGS, TOY PLANE MUSIC, ROUND HILL SONGS,
WB MUSIC CORP., UPPER DEC, ROC NATION MUSIC, MUSIC FAMAMANEM, NORTHSIDE INDEPENDENT MUSIC PUBLISHING LLC,
UNIVERSAL MUSIC CORP. and DRY RAIN ENTERTAINMENT
All Rights for BMG FIREFLY, MARSFORCE MUSIC, BMG GOLD SONGS and TOY PLANE MUSIC Administered by
BMG RIGHTS MANAGEMENT (US) LLC
All Rights for UPPER DEC, ROC NATION MUSIC and MUSIC FAMAMANEM Administered by WB MUSIC CORP.
All Rights for DRY RAIN ENTERTAINMENT Controlled and Administered by UNIVERSAL MUSIC CORP.
All Rights Reserved   Used by Permission

LIPS OF AN ANGEL

Clarinet

Words and Music by AUSTIN WINKLER,
ROSS HANSON, LLOYD GARVEY, MARK KING,
MICHAEL RODDEN and BRIAN HOWES

© 2005 EMI BLACKWOOD MUSIC INC., HINDER MUSIC CO. and HIGH BUCK PUBLISHING
All Rights Controlled and Administered by EMI BLACKWOOD MUSIC INC.
All Rights Reserved   International Copyright Secured   Used by Permission

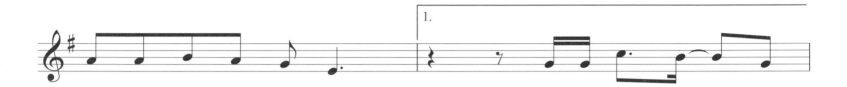

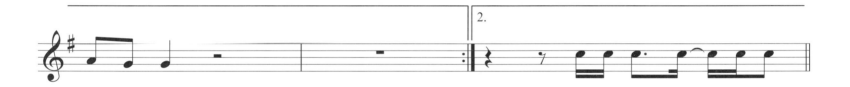

LITTLE TALKS

CLARINET

Words and Music by
OF MONSTERS AND MEN

Moderately

Copyright © 2012 Sony/ATV Music Publishing LLC, NannaBH Music and Mussi Music
All Rights Administered by Sony/ATV Music Publishing LLC, 424 Church Street, Suite 1200, Nashville, TN 37219
International Copyright Secured   All Rights Reserved

LET IT GO

CLARINET

Words and Music by JAMES BAY
and PAUL BARRY

Copyright © 2014 B-Unique Music Limited and Metrophonic Music Ltd.
All Rights for B-Unique Music Limited Administered Worldwide by Songs Of Kobalt Music Publishing
All Rights for Metrophonic Music Ltd. in the U.S. and Canada Administered by Universal - PolyGram International Publishing, Inc.
All Rights Reserved   Used by Permission

NEED YOU NOW

CLARINET

Words and Music by HILLARY SCOTT,
CHARLES KELLEY, DAVE HAYWOOD
and JOSH KEAR

© 2009 EMI FORAY MUSIC, HILLARY DAWN SONGS, WARNER-TAMERLANE PUBLISHING CORP., RADIOBULLETSPUBLISHING,
DWHAYWOOD MUSIC and ROUND HILL SONGS JOSH KEAR
All Rights for HILLARY DAWN SONGS Controlled and Administered by EMI FORAY MUSIC
All Rights for RADIOBULLETSPUBLISHING and DWHAYWOOD MUSIC Administered by WARNER-TAMERLANE PUBLISHING CORP.
All Rights Reserved   International Copyright Secured   Used by Permission

LOSING MY RELIGION

CLARINET

Words and Music by WILLIAM BERRY,
PETER BUCK, MICHAEL MILLS
and MICHAEL STIPE

Copyright © 1991 NIGHT GARDEN MUSIC
All Rights Administered by SONGS OF UNIVERSAL, INC.
All Rights Reserved   Used by Permission

99

LOVE SONG

CLARINET

Words and Music by
SARA BAREILLES

Copyright © 2006 Sony/ATV Music Publishing LLC and Tiny Bear Music
All Rights Administered by Sony/ATV Music Publishing LLC, 424 Church Street, Suite 1200, Nashville, TN 37219
International Copyright Secured   All Rights Reserved

Fine

D.S. al Fine

LOVE STORY

CLARINET

Words and Music by
TAYLOR SWIFT

Copyright © 2008 Sony/ATV Music Publishing LLC and Taylor Swift Music
All Rights Administered by Sony/ATV Music Publishing LLC, 424 Church Street, Suite 1200, Nashville, TN 37219
International Copyright Secured   All Rights Reserved

MORE THAN WORDS

Clarinet

Words and Music by NUNO BETTENCOURT
and GARY CHERONE

Copyright © 1990 COLOR ME BLIND MUSIC
All Rights Administered by ALMO MUSIC CORP.
All Rights Reserved   Used by Permission

NO ONE

CLARINET

Words and Music by ALICIA KEYS,
KERRY BROTHERS, JR. and GEORGE HARRY

Moderately

© 2007 EMI APRIL MUSIC INC., LELLOW PRODUCTIONS, BOOK OF DANIEL, UNIVERSAL MUSIC CORP. and D HARRY PRODUCTIONS
All Rights for LELLOW PRODUCTIONS and BOOK OF DANIEL Controlled and Administered by EMI APRIL MUSIC INC.
All Rights for D HARRY PRODUCTIONS Controlled and Administered by UNIVERSAL MUSIC CORP.
All Rights Reserved   International Copyright Secured   Used by Permission

To Coda ⊕

D.S. al Coda

CODA

100 YEARS

Clarinet

Words and Music by
JOHN ONDRASIK

Copyright © 2003 EMI Blackwood Music Inc. and Five For Fighting Music
All Rights Administered by Sony/ATV Music Publishing LLC, 424 Church Street, Suite 1200, Nashville, TN 37219
International Copyright Secured   All Rights Reserved

REHAB

Clarinet

Words and Music by
AMY WINEHOUSE

© 2006 EMI MUSIC PUBLISHING LTD.
All Rights in the U.S. and Canada Controlled and Administered by EMI BLACKWOOD MUSIC INC.
All Rights Reserved   International Copyright Secured   Used by Permission

THE POWER OF LOVE

Clarinet

Words by MARY SUSAN APPLEGATE
and JENNIFER RUSH
Music by CANDY DEROUGE
and GUNTHER MENDE

© 1986 EMI SONGS MUSIKVERLAG GMBH
All Rights for the U.S.A. and Canada Controlled and Administered by EMI APRIL MUSIC INC.
All Rights Reserved   International Copyright Secured   Used by Permission

ROAR

CLARINET

Words and Music by KATY PERRY,
LUKASZ GOTTWALD, MAX MARTIN,
BONNIE McKEE and HENRY WALTER

Moderately

© 2013 WB MUSIC CORP., WHEN I'M RICH YOU'LL BE MY BITCH, SONGS OF PULSE RECORDING, PRESCRIPTION SONGS,
BONNIE McKEE MUSIC, WHERE DA KASZ AT?, MXM MUSIC AB, KASZ MONEY PUBLISHING and ONEIROLOGY PUBLISHING
All Rights for WHEN I'M RICH YOU'LL BE MY BITCH Administered by WB MUSIC CORP.
All Rights for PRESCRIPTION SONGS, MXM MUSIC AB, KASZ MONEY PUBLISHING and ONEIROLOGY PUBLISHING
Administered by KOBALT SONGS MUSIC PUBLISHING
All Rights for BONNIE McKEE MUSIC and WHERE DA KASZ AT? Administered by SONGS OF KOBALT MUSIC PUBLISHING
All Rights Reserved   Used by Permission

ROLLING IN THE DEEP

Clarinet

Words and Music by ADELE ADKINS
and PAUL EPWORTH

Copyright © 2010, 2011 MELTED STONE PUBLISHING LTD. and EMI MUSIC PUBLISHING LTD.
All Rights for MELTED STONE PUBLISHING LTD. in the U.S. and Canada Controlled and Administered by
UNIVERSAL - SONGS OF POLYGRAM INTERNATIONAL, INC.
All Rights for EMI MUSIC PUBLISHING LTD. Administered by SONY/ATV MUSIC PUBLISHING LLC, 424 Church Street, Suite 1200, Nashville, TN 37219
All Rights Reserved   Used by Permission

ROYALS

CLARINET

Words and Music by ELLA YELICH-O'CONNOR
and JOEL LITTLE

Moderately

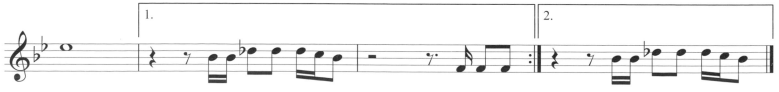

Copyright © 2012, 2013 Songs Music Publishing, LLC o/b/o Songs Of SMP and EMI April Music Inc.
All Rights on behalf of EMI April Music Inc. Administered by Sony/ATV Music Publishing LLC, 424 Church Street, Suite 1200, Nashville, TN 37219
All Rights Reserved   Used by Permission

SAVE THE BEST FOR LAST

Clarinet

Words and Music by WENDY WALDMAN,
PHIL GALDSTON and JON LIND

Copyright © 1989 EMI Longitude Music, Moon And Stars Music, Kazzoom Music, Inc. and Big Mystique Music
All Rights on behalf of EMI Longitude Music and Moon And Stars Music Administered by
Sony/ATV Music Publishing LLC, 424 Church Street, Suite 1200, Nashville, TN 37219
All Rights on behalf of Kazzoom Music, Inc. Administered by Imagem Music, LLC
All Rights on behalf of Big Mystique Music Administered by Kobalt Songs Music Publishing
International Copyright Secured   All Rights Reserved

SAY SOMETHING

Clarinet

Words and Music by IAN AXEL,
CHAD VACCARINO and MIKE CAMPBELL

Very slowly, in 4

Copyright © 2011 SONGS OF UNIVERSAL, INC., IAN AXEL MUSIC, CHAD VACCARINO PUBLISHING,
MANHATTAN ASTRONAUT MUSIC and RESERVOIR 416
All Rights for IAN AXEL MUSIC and CHAD VACCARINO PUBLISHING Controlled and Administered by SONGS OF UNIVERSAL, INC.
All Rights for MANHATTAN ASTRONAUT MUSIC and RESERVOIR 416 Administered by RESERVOIR MEDIA MANAGEMENT, INC.
All Rights Reserved   Used by Permission

SHAKE IT OFF

CLARINET

Words and Music by TAYLOR SWIFT,
MAX MARTIN and SHELLBACK

Copyright © 2014 Sony/ATV Music Publishing LLC, Taylor Swift Music and MXM
All Rights on behalf of Sony/ATV Music Publishing LLC and Taylor Swift Music Administered by
Sony/ATV Music Publishing LLC, 424 Church Street, Suite 1200, Nashville, TN 37219
All Rights on behalf of MXM Administered Worldwide by Kobalt Songs Music Publishing
International Copyright Secured All Rights Reserved

SECRETS

CLARINET

Words and Music by
RYAN TEDDER

Copyright © 2009 Sony/ATV Music Publishing LLC, Velvet Hammer Music and Midnite Miracle Music
All Rights Administered by Sony/ATV Music Publishing LLC, 424 Church Street, Suite 1200, Nashville, TN 37219
International Copyright Secured   All Rights Reserved

SHE WILL BE LOVED

CLARINET

Words and Music by ADAM LEVINE
and JAMES VALENTINE

Copyright © 2002 by Universal Music - MGB Songs, Valentine Valentine, Universal Music - Careers and February Twenty Second Music
All Rights for Valentine Valentine in the United States Administered by Universal Music - MGB Songs
All Rights for February Twenty Second Music in the United States Administered by Universal Music - Careers
International Copyright Secured   All Rights Reserved

SMELLS LIKE TEEN SPIRIT

Clarinet

Words and Music by KURT COBAIN,
KRIST NOVOSELIC and DAVE GROHL

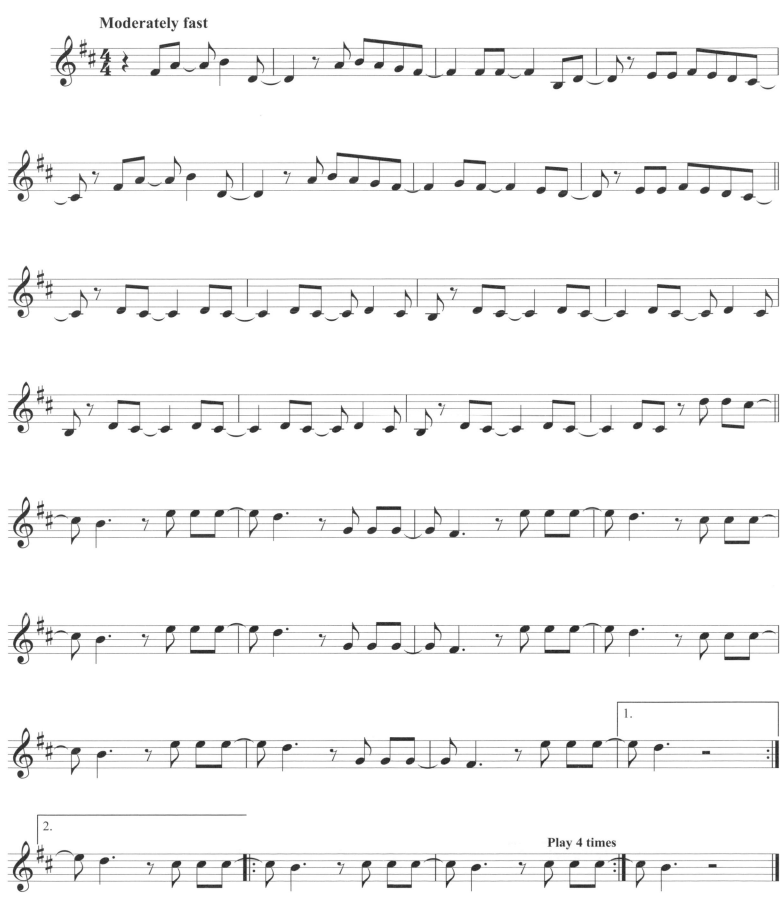

Copyright © 1991 The End Of Music, Primary Wave Tunes, M.J. Twelve Music and Murky Slough Music
All Rights for The End Of Music and Primary Wave Tunes Administered by BMG Rights Management (US) LLC
All Rights Reserved   Used by Permission

SOMETHING TO TALK ABOUT
(Let's Give Them Something to Talk About)

CLARINET

Words and Music by
SHIRLEY EIKHARD

Moderately

© 1985, 1988 EMI BLACKWOOD MUSIC INC. and CANVEE MUSIC
All Rights Reserved   International Copyright Secured   Used by Permission

STAY WITH ME

Clarinet

Words and Music by SAM SMITH,
JAMES NAPIER, WILLIAM EDWARD PHILLIPS,
TOM PETTY and JEFF LYNNE

Copyright © 2014 Sony/ATV Music Publishing (UK) Limited, Naughty Words Limited, Stellar Songs Ltd., Salli Isaak Songs, Ltd.,
Method Paperwork Ltd., Gone Gator Music and EMI April Music Inc.
All Rights on behalf of Sony/ATV Music Publishing (UK) Limited, Naughty Words Limited, Stellar Songs Ltd. and EMI April Music Inc.
Administered by Sony/ATV Music Publishing LLC, 424 Church Street, Suite 1200, Nashville, TN 37219
All Rights on behalf of Salli Isaak Songs Ltd. and Method Paperwork Ltd. in the U.S. and Canada Administered by
Universal - PolyGram International Tunes, Inc.
International Copyright Secured   All Rights Reserved

STACY'S MOM

CLARINET

Words and Music by CHRIS COLLINGWOOD
and ADAM SCHLESINGER

© 2003 Monkey Demon Music (BMI) and Vaguely Familiar Music (ASCAP)
International Copyright Secured   All Rights Reserved

STAY

CLARINET

Words and Music by MIKKY EKKO
and JUSTIN PARKER

Copyright © 2012 Sony/ATV Music Publishing LLC, Sony/ATV Music Publishing UK Limited and Kkids And Stray Dogs
All Rights Administered by Sony/ATV Music Publishing LLC, 424 Church Street, Suite 1200, Nashville, TN 37219
International Copyright Secured   All Rights Reserved

Fine

D.S. al Fine

STRONGER
(What Doesn't Kill You)

Clarinet

Words and Music by GREG KURSTIN,
JORGEN ELOFSSON, DAVID GAMSON
and ALEXANDRA TAMPOSI

Moderately

© 2011 EMI APRIL MUSIC INC., KURSTIN MUSIC, UNIVERSAL MUSIC PUBLISHING MGB SCANDINAVIA,
BMG GOLD SONGS and PERFECT STORM MUSIC GROUP AB
All Rights for KURSTIN MUSIC Controlled and Administered by EMI APRIL MUSIC INC.
All Rights for UNIVERSAL MUSIC PUBLISHING MGB SCANDINAVIA in the United States and Canada
Administered by UNIVERSAL MUSIC - CAREERS
All Rights for BMG GOLD SONGS Administered by BMG RIGHTS MANAGEMENT (US) LLC
All Rights for PERFECT STORM MUSIC GROUP AB Administered by SONY/ATV MUSIC PUBLISHING LLC, 424 Church Street, Suite 1200, Nashville, TN 37219
All Rights Reserved   International Copyright Secured   Used by Permission

2nd time, to Coda ⊕
3rd time, Fine

D.S. al Coda

CODA ⊕

D.S. al Fine

TEARS IN HEAVEN

CLARINET

Words and Music by ERIC CLAPTON
and WILL JENNINGS

Copyright © 1992 by E.C. Music Ltd. and Blue Sky Rider Songs
All Rights for Blue Sky Rider Songs Administered by Irving Music, Inc.
International Copyright Secured   All Rights Reserved

TEENAGE DREAM

Clarinet

Words and Music by KATY PERRY,
BONNIE McKEE, LUKASZ GOTTWALD,
MAX MARTIN and BENJAMIN LEVIN

Moderately

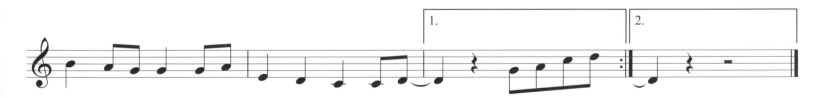

© 2010 WHEN I'M RICH YOU'LL BE MY BITCH, BONNIE McKEE MUSIC, DOWNTOWN DMP SONGS, SONGS OF PULSE RECORDING,
KASZ MONEY PUBLISHING, MARATONE AB, PRESCRIPTION SONGS, LLC and WHERE DA KASZ AT?
All Rights for WHEN I'M RICH YOU'LL BE MY BITCH Administered by WB MUSIC CORP.
All Rights for BONNIE McKEE MUSIC and DOWNTOWN DMP SONGS Administered by DOWNTOWN MUSIC PUBLISHING LLC
All Rights for KASZ MONEY PUBLISHING, MARATONE AB, PRESCRIPTION SONGS, LLC and WHERE DA KASZ AT?
Administered by KOBALT MUSIC PUBLISHING AMERICA, INC.
All Rights Reserved   Used by Permission

THINKING OUT LOUD

CLARINET

Words and Music by ED SHEERAN
and AMY WADGE

Moderately slow

Copyright © 2014 Sony/ATV Music Publishing Limited UK and BDI Music Ltd.
All Rights on behalf of Sony/ATV Music Publishing Limited UK Administered by Sony/ATV Music Publishing LLC, 424 Church Street, Suite 1200, Nashville, TN 37219
International Copyright Secured   All Rights Reserved

THIS LOVE

CLARINET

Words and Music by ADAM LEVINE
and JESSE CARMICHAEL

Copyright © 2002 by Universal Music - MGB Songs, Valentine Valentine, Universal Music - Careers and February Twenty Second Music
All Rights for Valentine Valentine in the United States Administered by Universal Music - MGB Songs
All Rights for February Twenty Second Music in the United States Administered by Universal Music - Careers
International Copyright Secured   All Rights Reserved

A THOUSAND YEARS

from the Summit Entertainment film THE TWILIGHT SAGE: BREAKING DAWN - PART 1

Clarinet

Words and Music by DAVID HODGES
and CHRISTINA PERRI

© 2001 EMI BLACKWOOD MUSIC INC., 12:06 PUBLISHING, MISS PERRI LANE PUBLISHING and
WARNER-TAMERLANE PUBLISHING CORP.
All Rights for 12:06 PUBLISHING Controlled and Administered by EMI BLACKWOOD MUSIC INC.
All Rights for MISS PERRI LANE PUBLISHING Controlled and Administered by SONGS OF KOBALT MUSIC PUBLISHING
All Rights Reserved International Copyright Secured Used by Permission

TILL THE WORLD ENDS

CLARINET

Words and Music by LUKASZ GOTTWALD,
MAX MARTIN, KESHA SEBERT
and ALEXANDER KRONLUND

Moderately fast

Copyright © 2011 Kasz Money Publishing, Maratone AB, Dynamite Cop Music and WB Music Corp.
All Rights for Kasz Money Publishing, Maratone AB and Dynamite Cop Music Administered by Kobalt Music Publishing America, Inc.
All Rights Reserved   Used by Permission

UPTOWN FUNK

CLARINET

Words and Music by MARK RONSON,
BRUNO MARS, PHILIP LAWRENCE, JEFF BHASKER, DEVON GALLASPY,
NICHOLAUS WILLIAMS, LONNIE SIMMONS, RONNIE WILSON,
CHARLES WILSON, RUDOLPH TAYLOR and ROBERT WILSON

Copyright © 2014 by Songs of Zelig, Imagem CV, BMG Gold Songs, Mars Force Music, WB Music Corp., Thou Art The Hunger,
ZZR Music LLC, Sony/ATV Songs LLC, Way Above Music, Sony/ATV Ballad, TIG7 Publishing,
Trinlanta Publishing and Taking Care Of Business Music, Inc.
All Rights for Songs Of Zelig and Imagem CV Administered by Songs Of Imagem Music
All Rights for BMG Gold Songs and Mars Force Music Administered by BMG Rights Management (US) LLC
All Rights for Thou Art The Hunger Administered by WB Music Corp.
All Rights for ZZR Music LLC Administered by Universal Music Corp.
All Rights for Sony/ATV Songs LLC, Way Above Music and Sony/ATV Ballad Administered by
Sony/ATV Music Publishing LLC, 424 Church Street, Suite 1200, Nashville, TN 37219
All Rights Reserved Used by Permission
- interpolates "All Gold Everything" performed by Trinidad James © 2015 Songs Music Publishing, LLC o/b/o Trinlanta Publishing,
TIG7 Publishing LLC and Songs MP, used with permission

VIVA LA VIDA

Clarinet

Words and Music by GUY BERRYMAN,
JON BUCKLAND, WILL CHAMPION
and CHRIS MARTIN

Copyright © 2008 by Universal Music Publishing MGB Ltd.
All Rights in the United States and Canada Administered by Universal Music - MGB Songs
International Copyright Secured   All Rights Reserved

WAITING ON THE WORLD TO CHANGE

CLARINET

Words and Music by
JOHN MAYER

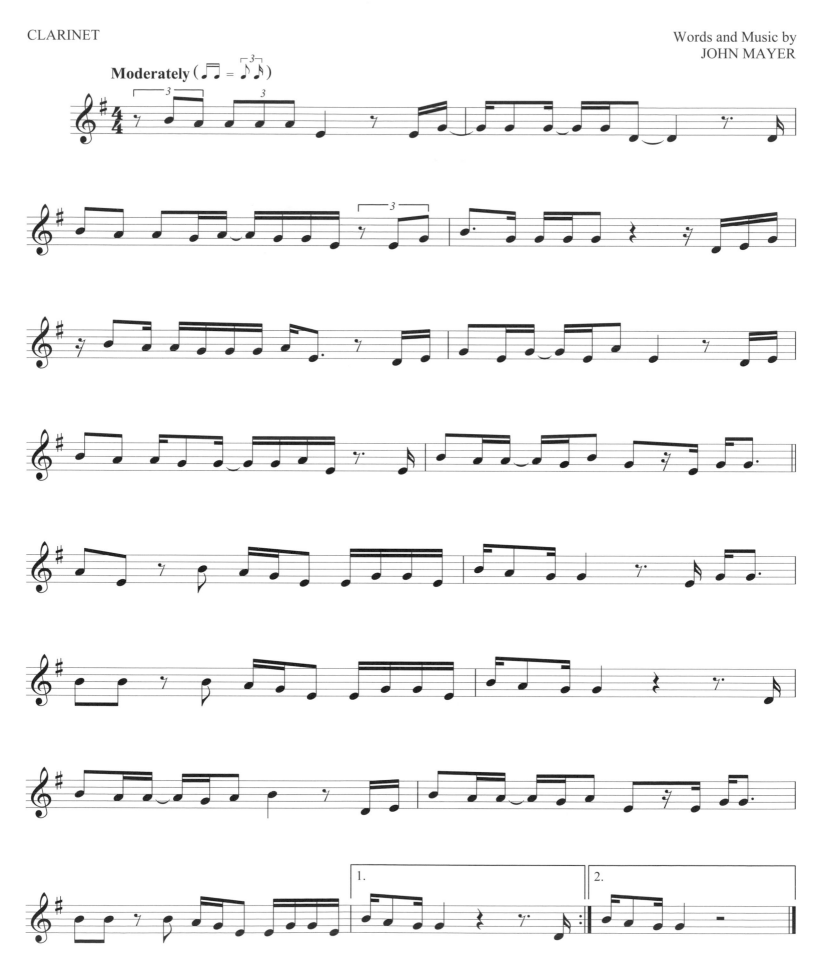

Copyright © 2006 Specific Harm Music
All Rights Administered by Goodium Music, Inc., c/o Cal Financial Group, 700 Harris Street, Suite 201, Charlottesville, VA 22903
International Copyright Secured   All Rights Reserved

WE CAN'T STOP

Clarinet

Words and Music by MILEY CYRUS,
THERON THOMAS, TIMOTHY THOMAS, MICHAEL WILLIAMS,
PIERRE SLAUGHTER, DOUGLAS DAVIS and RICKY WALTERS

Copyright © 2013 SUGA BEAR RECORDZ PUBLISHING, UNIVERSAL MUSIC CORP., T.N.T. EXPLOSIVE PUBLISHING, WB MUSIC CORP.,
SOUNDS FROM EARDRUMMERS LLC, WARNER-TAMERLANE PUBLISHING STORP., EARDRUMMERS MUSIC PUBLISHING LLC,
PIERRE SLAUGHTER PUBLISHING DESIGNEE, ENTERTAINING MUSIC and SLICK RICK MUSIC CORP.
All Rights for SUGA BEAR RECORDZ PUBLISHING Controlled and Administered by SONGS OF UNIVERSAL, INC.
All Rights for T.N.T. EXPLOSIVE PUBLISHING Controlled and Administered by UNIVERSAL MUSIC CORP.
All Rights for SOUNDS FROM EARDRUMMERS LLC Administered by WB MUSIC CORP.
All Rights for EARDRUMMERS MUSIC PUBLISHING LLC and PIERRE SLAUGHTER PUBLISHING DESIGNEE
Administered by WARNER-TAMERLANE PUBLISHING CORP.
All Rights Reserved   Used by Permission

WE BELONG TOGETHER

CLARINET

Words and Music by MARIAH CAREY,
JERMAINE DUPRI, MANUEL SEAL, JOHNTA AUSTIN,
DARNELL BRISTOL, KENNETH EDMONDS, SIDNEY JOHNSON,
PATRICK MOTEN, BOBBY WOMACK and SANDRA SULLY

Slow Soul

Copyright © 2005 RYE SONGS, UNIVERSAL MUSIC - MGB SONGS, SLACK A.D. MUSIC, BMG MONARCH, NAKED UNDER MY CLOTHES,
EMI APRIL MUSIC INC., SHANIAH CYMONE MUSIC, SONY/ATV MUSIC PUBLISHING LLC, HIP CHIC MUSIC, ECAF MUSIC,
MISTER JOHNSON'S JAMS MUSIC, INC., WARNER-TAMERLANE PUBLISHING CORP., ABKO MUSIC, INC. and BALLADS BY DESIGN
All Rights for RYE SONGS Controlled and Administered by SONGS OF UNIVERSAL, INC.
All Rights for SLACK A.D. MUSIC Controlled and Administered by UNIVERSAL MUSIC - MGB SONGS
All Rights for BMG MONARCH and NAKED UNDER MY CLOTHES Administered by BMG RIGHTS MANAGEMENT (US) LLC
All Rights for EMI APRIL MUSIC INC., SHANIAH CYMONE MUSIC, SONY/ATV MUSIC PUBLISHING LLC, HIP CHIC MUSIC, ECAF MUSIC
and MISTER JOHNSON'S JAMS MUSIC, INC.Administered by SONY/ATV MUSIC PUBLISHING LLC, 424 Church Street, Suite 1200, Nashville, TN 37219
All Rights Reserved   Used by Permission
- contains elements of "Two Occasions" by Darnell Bristol, Kenneth Edmonds and Sidney Johnson
and "If You Think You're Lonely Now" by Patrick Moten, Bobby Womack and Sandra Sully

WE FOUND LOVE

Clarinet

Words and Music by
CALVIN HARRIS

© 2011 EMI MUSIC PUBLISHING LTD.
All Rights for the U.S. and Canada Controlled and Administered by EMI APRIL MUSIC INC.
All Rights Reserved   International Copyright Secured   Used by Permission

WHAT MAKES YOU BEAUTIFUL

Clarinet

Words and Music by SAVAN KOTECHA,
RAMI YACOUB and CARL FALK

Copyright © 2011, 2015 EMI April Music Inc., Kobalt Music Copyrights SARL and BMG Rights Management Scandinavia AB
All Rights on behalf of EMI April Music Inc. Administered by Sony/ATV Music Publishing LLC, 424 Church Street, Suite 1200, Nashville, TN 37219
All Rights on behalf of BMG Rights Management Scandinavia AB Administered by BMG Rights Management (US) LLC
All Rights Reserved   Used by Permission

WHEN YOU SAY NOTHING AT ALL

Clarinet

Words and Music by DON SCHLITZ
and PAUL OVERSTREET

Copyright © 1988 UNIVERSAL MUSIC CORP., DON SCHLITZ MUSIC, SCREEN GEMS-EMI MUSIC INC. and SCARLET MOON MUSIC, INC.
All Rights for DON SCHLITZ MUSIC Controlled and Administered by UNIVERSAL MUSIC CORP.
All Rights for SCREEN GEMS-EMI MUSIC INC. Administered by Sony/ATV Music Publishing LLC, 424 Church Street, Suite 1200, Nashville, TN 37219
All Rights for SCARLET MOON MUSIC, INC. Administered Worldwide by KOBALT MUSIC GROUP LTD.
All Rights Reserved   Used by Permission

YOU RAISE ME UP

Clarinet

Words and Music by BRENDAN GRAHAM
and ROLF LOVLAND

Copyright © 2002 by Peermusic (UK) Ltd. and Universal Music Publishing, A Division of Universal Music AS
All Rights for Peermusic (UK) Ltd. in the United States Controlled and Administered by Peermusic III, Ltd.
All Rights for Universal Music Publishing, A Division of Universal Music AS in the United States and Canada Controlled and Administered by
Universal - PolyGram International Publishing, Inc. (Publishing) and Alfred Music (Print)
International Copyright Secured   All Rights Reserved

YEAH!

CLARINET

Words and Music by JAMES PHILLIPS,
LA MARQUIS JEFFERSON, CHRISTOPHER BRIDGES,
JONATHAN SMITH and SEAN GARRETT

Moderately

Copyright © 2004 EMI April Music Inc., Ludacris Music Publishing Inc., Air Control Music, Basajamba Music, Me And Marq Music,
Christopher Garrett's Publishing, Hitco South, Christopher Matthew Music, Hitco Music and Reservoir 416
All Rights on behalf of EMI April Music Inc., Ludacris Music Publishing Inc., Air Control Music and Basajamba Music Administered by
Sony/ATV Music Publishing LLC, 424 Church Street, Suite 1200, Nashville, TN 37219
All Rights on behalf of Me And Marq Music, Christopher Garrett's Publishing, Hitco South, Christopher Matthew Music
and Hitco Music Administered by BMG Rights Management (US) LLC
All Rights on behalf of Reservoir 416 Administered by Reservoir Media Management, Inc.
International Copyright Secured   All Rights Reserved

YOU WERE MEANT FOR ME

Clarinet

Words and Music by JEWEL MURRAY
and STEVE POLTZ

© 1995, 1996 WIGGLY TOOTH MUSIC and THIRD STORY MUSIC, INC.
All Rights for WIGGLY TOOTH MUSIC Administered by DCTM AVE/DOWNTOWN MUSIC PUBLISHING LLC
Worldwide Rights for THIRD STORY MUSIC, INC. owned by ARC/CONRAD MUSIC LLC
All Rights for ARC/CONRAD MUSIC LLC Administered by BMG RIGHTS MANAGEMENT (US) LLC
All Rights Reserved   Used by Permission

153

YOU'RE BEAUTIFUL

Clarinet

Words and Music by JAMES BLUNT,
SACHA SKARBEK and AMANDA GHOST

Copyright © 2005 EMI Music Publishing Ltd., Universal Music Publishing Ltd. and Bucks Music Ltd.
All Rights on behalf of EMI Music Publishing Ltd. Administered by Sony/ATV Music Publishing LLC, 424 Church Street, Suite 1200, Nashville, TN 37219
All Rights on behalf of Universal Music Publishing Ltd. in the U.S. and Canada Controlled and Administered by Universal - Songs Of PolyGram International, Inc.
All Rights on behalf of Bucks Music Ltd. in the U.S. Administered by David Platz Music (USA) Inc.
International Copyright Secured   All Rights Reserved

YOU'RE STILL THE ONE

Clarinet

Words and Music by SHANIA TWAIN
and R.J. LANGE

Copyright © 1997 LOON ECHO, INC. and OUT OF POCKET PRODUCTIONS, LTD.
All Rights for LOON ECHO, INC. Controlled and Administered by SONGS OF UNIVERSAL, INC.
All Rights for OUT OF POCKET PRODUCTIONS, LTD. in the U.S. and Canada Administered by UNIVERSAL - POLYGRAM INTERNATIONAL PUBLISHING, INC.
All Rights Reserved   Used by Permission

YOU'VE GOT A FRIEND IN ME

from Walt Disney's TOY STORY

CLARINET

Music and Lyrics by
RANDY NEWMAN

Easy Shuffle

© 1995 Walt Disney Music Company
All Rights Reserved.   Used by Permission.

101 SONGS

BIG COLLECTIONS OF FAVORITE SONGS ARRANGED FOR SOLO INSTRUMENTALISTS.

101 BROADWAY SONGS

00154199	Flute	$15.99
00154200	Clarinet	$15.99
00154201	Alto Sax	$15.99
00154202	Tenor Sax	$16.99
00154203	Trumpet	$15.99
00154204	Horn	$15.99
00154205	Trombone	$15.99
00154206	Violin	$15.99

00154207 Viola......$15.99
00154208 Cello......$15.99

101 DISNEY SONGS

00244104	Flute	$17.99
00244106	Clarinet	$17.99
00244107	Alto Sax	$17.99
00244108	Tenor Sax	$17.99
00244109	Trumpet	$17.99
00244112	Horn	$17.99
00244120	Trombone	$17.99
00244121	Violin	$17.99

00244125 Viola......$17.99
00244126 Cello......$17.99

101 MOVIE HITS

00158087	Flute	$15.99
00158088	Clarinet	$15.99
00158089	Alto Sax	$15.99
00158090	Tenor Sax	$15.99
00158091	Trumpet	$15.99
00158092	Horn	$15.99
00158093	Trombone	$15.99
00158094	Violin	$15.99

00158095 Viola......$15.99
00158096 Cello......$15.99

101 CHRISTMAS SONGS

00278637	Flute	$15.99
00278638	Clarinet	$15.99
00278639	Alto Sax	$15.99
00278640	Tenor Sax	$15.99
00278641	Trumpet	$15.99
00278642	Horn	$14.99
00278643	Trombone	$15.99
00278644	Violin	$15.99

00278645 Viola......$15.99
00278646 Cello......$15.99

101 HIT SONGS

00194561	Flute	$17.99
00197182	Clarinet	$17.99
00197183	Alto Sax	$17.99
00197184	Tenor Sax	$17.99
00197185	Trumpet	$17.99
00197186	Horn	$17.99
00197187	Trombone	$17.99
00197188	Violin	$17.99

00197189 Viola......$17.99
00197190 Cello......$17.99

101 POPULAR SONGS

00224722	Flute	$17.99
00224723	Clarinet	$17.99
00224724	Alto Sax	$17.99
00224725	Tenor Sax	$17.99
00224726	Trumpet	$17.99
00224727	Horn	$17.99
00224728	Trombone	$17.99
00224729	Violin	$17.99

00224730 Viola......$17.99
00224731 Cello......$17.99

101 CLASSICAL THEMES

00155315	Flute	$15.99
00155317	Clarinet	$15.99
00155318	Alto Sax	$15.99
00155319	Tenor Sax	$15.99
00155320	Trumpet	$15.99
00155321	Horn	$15.99
00155322	Trombone	$15.99
00155323	Violin	$15.99

00155324 Viola......$15.99
00155325 Cello......$15.99

101 JAZZ SONGS

00146363	Flute	$15.99
00146364	Clarinet	$15.99
00146366	Alto Sax	$15.99
00146367	Tenor Sax	$15.99
00146368	Trumpet	$15.99
00146369	Horn	$14.99
00146370	Trombone	$15.99
00146371	Violin	$15.99

00146372 Viola......$15.99
00146373 Cello......$15.99

101 MOST BEAUTIFUL SONGS

00291023	Flute	$16.99
00291041	Clarinet	$16.99
00291042	Alto Sax	$17.99
00291043	Tenor Sax	$17.99
00291044	Trumpet	$16.99
00291045	Horn	$16.99
00291046	Trombone	$16.99
00291047	Violin	$16.99

00291048 Viola......$16.99
00291049 Cello......$17.99

See complete song lists and sample pages at www.halleonard.com

HAL•LEONARD®
www.halleonard.com

Prices, contents and availability subject to change without notice.

101 TIPS FROM HAL LEONARD

STUFF ALL THE PROS KNOW AND USE

Ready to take your skills to the next level? These books present valuable how-to insight that musicians of all styles and levels can benefit from. The text, photos, music, diagrams and accompanying audio provide a terrific, easy-to-use resource for a variety of topics.

101 HAMMOND B-3 TIPS
by Brian Charette
Topics include: funky scales and modes; unconventional harmonies; creative chord voicings; cool drawbar settings; ear-grabbing special effects; professional gigging advice; practicing effectively; making good use of the pedals; and much more!
00128918 Book/Online Audio $14.99

101 HARMONICA TIPS
by Steve Cohen
Topics include: techniques, position playing, soloing, accompaniment, the blues, equipment, performance, maintenance, and much more!
00821040 Book/Online Audio $17.99

101 CELLO TIPS—2ND EDITION
by Angela Schmidt
Topics include: bowing techniques, non-classical playing, electric cellos, accessories, gig tips, practicing, recording and much more!
00149094 Book/Online Audio $14.99

101 FLUTE TIPS
by Elaine Schmidt
Topics include: selecting the right flute for you, finding the right teacher, warm-up exercises, practicing effectively, taking good care of your flute, gigging advice, staying and playing healthy, and much more.
00119883 Book/CD Pack..................................$14.99

101 SAXOPHONE TIPS
by Eric Morones
Topics include: techniques; maintenance; equipment; practicing; recording; performance; and much more!
00311082 Book/CD Pack..................................$19.99

101 TRUMPET TIPS
by Scott Barnard
Topics include: techniques, articulation, tone production, soloing, exercises, special effects, equipment, performance, maintenance and much more.
00312082 Book/CD Pack..................................$14.99

101 UPRIGHT BASS TIPS
by Andy McKee
Topics include: right- and left-hand technique, improvising and soloing, practicing, proper care of the instrument, ear training, performance, and much more.
00102009 Book/Online Audio $14.99

101 BASS TIPS
by Gary Willis
Topics include: techniques, improvising and soloing, equipment, practicing, ear training, performance, theory, and much more.
00695542 Book/Online Audio $19.99

101 DRUM TIPS—2ND EDITION
Topics include: grooves, practicing, warming up, tuning, gear, performance, and much more!
00151936 Book/Online Audio $14.99

101 FIVE-STRING BANJO TIPS
by Fred Sokolow
Topics include: techniques, ear training, performance, and much more!
00696647 Book/CD Pack..................................$14.99

101 GUITAR TIPS
by Adam St. James
Topics include: scales, music theory, truss rod adjustments, proper recording studio set-ups, and much more. The book also features snippets of advice from some of the most celebrated guitarists and producers in the music business.
00695737 Book/Online Audio $17.99

101 MANDOLIN TIPS
by Fred Sokolow
Topics include: playing tips, practicing tips, accessories, mandolin history and lore, practical music theory, and much more!
00119493 Book/Online Audio $14.99

101 RECORDING TIPS
by Adam St. James
This book contains recording tips, suggestions, and advice learned firsthand from legendary producers, engineers, and artists. These tricks of the trade will improve anyone's home or pro studio recordings.
00311035 Book/CD Pack..................................$14.95

101 UKULELE TIPS
by Fred Sokolow with Ronny Schiff
Topics include: techniques, improvising and soloing, equipment, practicing, ear training, performance, uke history and lore, and much more!
00696596 Book/Online Audio $15.99

101 VIOLIN TIPS
by Angela Schmidt
Topics include: bowing techniques, non-classical playing, electric violins, accessories, gig tips, practicing, recording, and much more!
00842672 Book/CD Pack..................................$14.99

Prices, contents and availability subject to change without notice.

HAL•LEONARD®
www.halleonard.com